MW00826648

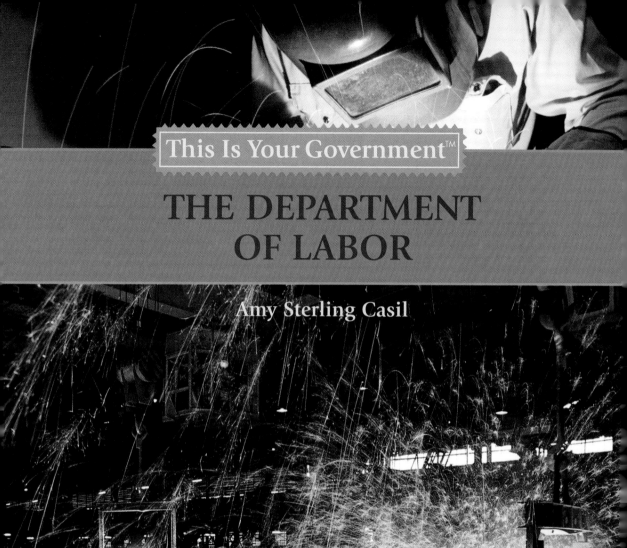

This Is Your Government™

THE DEPARTMENT OF LABOR

Amy Sterling Casil

rosen central™

The Rosen Publishing Group, Inc., New York

Published in 2006 by The Rosen Publishing Group, Inc.
29 East 21st Street, New York, NY 10010

Library of Congress Cataloging-in-Publication Data

Casil, Amy Sterling.
The Department of Labor/by Amy Sterling Casil.—1st ed.
    p. cm.—(This is your government)
Includes bibliographical references and index.
ISBN 1-4042-0210-2 (lib. bdg.)
ISBN 1-4042-0663-9 (pbk. bdg.)
1. United States. Dept. of Labor—Juvenile literature. 2. United States. Dept.
of Labor—History—Juvenile literature. 3. Labor—United States—History—
Juvenile literature
I. Title. II. Series.
HD8066.C28 2005
331'.0973—dc22

2004000187

Cover images: Left to right: William B. Wilson, Frances Perkins,
Ann Dore McLaughlin, Robert B. Reich, and Elaine L. Chao.

CONTENTS

Introduction

The United States Department of Labor is one of fifteen executive departments that advises the president on major subjects that are important to the safety, security, and prosperity of the United States. These departments are members of the presidential cabinet, an advisory group that dates back to the very beginnings of the presidency. Article II of the U.S. Constitution, signed on September 17, 1787, authorized the creation of some of these departments (such as the Treasury Department), while others have been added to the cabinet over the years (including the Department of Energy in 1977 and the Department of Homeland Security in 2002).

Each department is headed by a secretary. The president does not have the only say in creating cabinet departments or appointing their secretaries. Congress enacts legislation to create

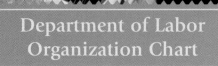

Department of Labor Organization Chart

CABINET MEMBERS

Secretary of Agriculture	Secretary of Commerce	Secretary of Defense	Secretary of Education	Secretary of Energy	Secretary of Health and Human Services	Secretary of Homeland Security	Secretary of Housing and Urban Development

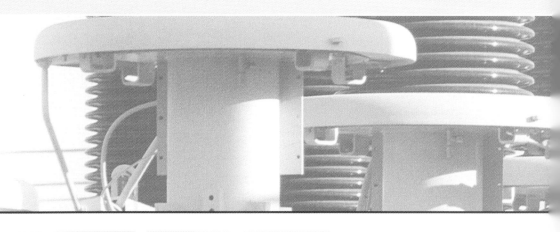

Office of Disability Employment Policy	Occupational Safety and Health Administration	Mine Safety and Health Administration	Employee Benefits Security Administration	Bureau of Labor Statistics	Pension Benefit Guaranty Corporation

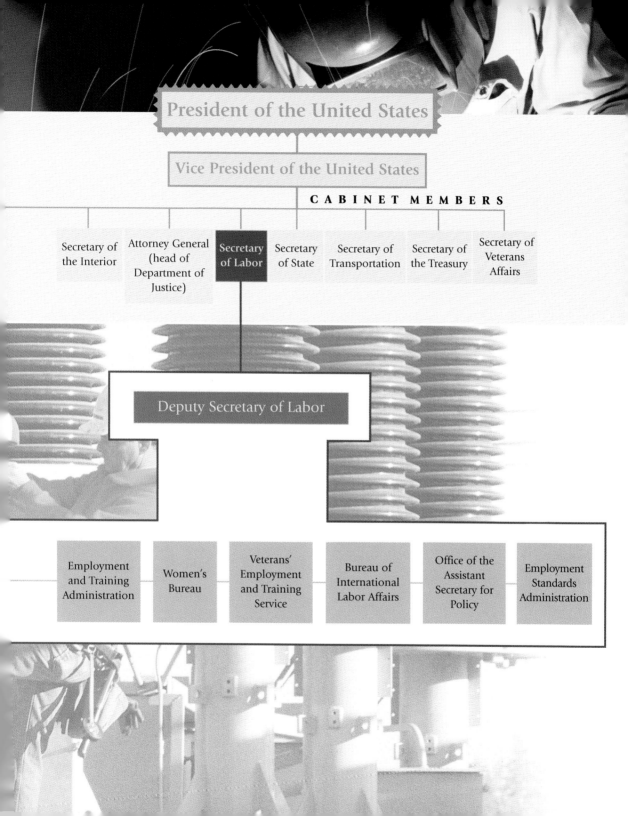

President of the United States

Vice President of the United States

CABINET MEMBERS

Secretary of the Interior

Attorney General (head of Department of Justice)

Secretary of Labor

Secretary of State

Secretary of Transportation

Secretary of the Treasury

Secretary of Veterans Affairs

Deputy Secretary of Labor

Employment and Training Administration

Women's Bureau

Veterans' Employment and Training Service

Bureau of International Labor Affairs

Office of the Assistant Secretary for Policy

Employment Standards Administration

cabinet-level departments, and the president's nominations for department secretaries are sent to the U.S. Senate for "advice and consent." The nation's first three cabinet secretaries were the heads of the Departments of Treasury, State, and War (now the Department of Defense).

Originally, the group that advised the president was not even called a cabinet. President James Madison used the word "cabinet" to describe the meetings he held with his department secretaries. Cabinet departments change as the United States itself changes. The newest cabinet-level department is the Department of Homeland Security, created by the Homeland Security Act of 2002. Tom Ridge was its first secretary. This new department was the first major reorganization of the U.S. cabinet since President Harry S. Truman merged the four branches of the U.S. armed forces into the Department of Defense in 1947.

An earlier, similar reorganization established the U.S. Department of Labor (DOL). Before the DOL was established, issues relating to employees were addressed by the Department of Commerce and Labor (created in 1903). This new department was charged with promoting the health of the economy and American business. The needs of businesses and their employees are often different, however, so in 1913, the Organic Act of the Department of Labor, signed into law by President William Howard Taft, established a separate and independent U.S. Department of Labor and a Department of Commerce.

The Organic Act of the Department of Labor stated that the purpose of the Department of Labor "shall be to foster, promote, and develop the welfare of the wage earners of the United States, to improve their working conditions, and to advance their opportunities for profitable employment." Today, the Department of Labor is responsible for these same activities and more. Its mission of promoting the welfare of workers and those seeking work has expanded to include protecting retirees and their retirement and health care benefits, helping employers find workers, and supporting negotiations between companies and their unionized workers. The department also tracks changes in employment, prices, and other national economic measurements in order to locate weak spots in the economy and to try to shore them up.

Before the DOL was created to help protect American workers, there was no such thing as a government-regulated minimum wage (the lowest amount of money employers can pay their workers per hour). Employers were free to pay workers very little. Sometimes workers were not paid at all, and they had almost no ability to have their complaints heard or improve their situations. People who lost their jobs had no one to turn to. Employers had all the power. There was no government organization to argue on behalf of workers or force companies to pay fair wages and ensure safe and healthy working conditions. There was no such thing as unemployment insurance, which

Two boys stand in front of a horse in a West Virginia coal mine in 1908. This photograph was taken by Lewis W. Hine, an investigative photographer for the National Child Labor Committee. From 1908 to 1912, Hine traveled throughout the United States, photographing children working long hours in factories, mines, and fields.

pays benefits to people who are laid off while they look for new jobs. Employers could discriminate against workers of certain races, ethnic groups, religions, genders, or sexual orientations. Unsafe working conditions were common in, for example, sweatshops, coal mines, and factories. Child labor was common, with children as young as eight years old working long hours in unsafe conditions. Kids who worked all day long had no time for school.

Before the creation of the DOL, there was not even a standard workday or week. Today, an eight-hour day and a forty-hour workweek are the standard. Those who are paid by the hour and who work more than forty hours a week now must receive overtime pay. Before the establishment of the DOL and the passage of a series of important labor laws, employees worked as long as they were needed, often far more than eight hours a day and forty hours a week, and they seldom received extra pay in return.

Today the DOL administers more than 180 federal laws covering workplace activities for more than 10 million employers and 125 million workers in the United States.

These laws cover:

- ✖ Workplace safety and health
- ✖ Wages and work hours
- ✖ Equal employment opportunity
- ✖ Agricultural workers
- ✖ Foreign workers
- ✖ Veterans' protections
- ✖ Government contracts
- ✖ Retirement and health benefits
- ✖ Whistle-blower protections (whistle-blowers are workers who
- ✖ report to the authorities on problems in the workplace)

From protecting the rights of older workers to enforcing rules about how much and when minors (children under age eighteen) can work, the Department of Labor eventually touches every American life. Chances are that someday you will be part of the nation's workforce, and someone you know is already working. Thanks to the Department of Labor, for most Americans, working in the United States today is safe and fair, and it pays a decent living wage.

CHAPTER ONE

The History of the Department of Labor

The establishment of a cabinet-level department focusing exclusively on American workers was the product of more than fifty years of effort on the part of the U.S. labor movement, also known as organized labor.

Organized labor is another name for labor unions. Labor unions got their start in the United States in the early 1800s. In local areas, skilled workers—such as carpenters and printers— began to join together to negotiate for better pay, working hours, and working conditions. By the mid-nineteenth century, the first national labor unions had formed.

One of the most famous union leaders, Samuel L. Gompers, became president of the American Federation of

Labor (AFL) in 1886. Under his leadership, the AFL began to use collective bargaining to gain benefits for its members. Collective bargaining is a technique in which union representatives negotiate with company owners on behalf of all their union members.

The Industrial Revolution

The history of the U.S. labor movement and the Department of Labor is tied to the many social and economic changes that are collectively referred to as the Industrial Revolution. Starting in the 1870s, the Industrial Revolution ushered in the nation's shift from an agriculture-based economy to one more reliant on mechanized manufacturing. At the same time, the population was growing rapidly. In 1860, the year before the Civil War began, the U.S. population was 31.5 million. By 1900, the population had grown to 76.2 million. Only ten years later, in 1910, there were more than 92 million people living in the United States.

As the population grew, so did the railroads, which expanded from 30,000 miles (48,280 kilometers) of track in 1860 to 270,000 miles (434,523 km) in 1900. Factories also sprang up everywhere. Before the Civil War, the only large factories were textile or cloth factories, mostly clustered in the Northeast. After the Civil War, many industries built large factories, using labor from the rapidly growing population—mostly

Samuel Gompers *(left)* was one of the founders of the American Federation of Labor (AFL) in 1886. He served as its president right up until his death in 1924. Under his leadership, the organization grew from a small number of struggling labor unions to become the dominant labor organization in the United States and Canada.

recent immigrants—to do the work. The large factories created an impersonal, noisy, and dangerous workplace. Skilled manual labor or tradesmen became less common as the factories introduced fast-paced and mechanized work that people had previously performed by hand. For example, a glassblower could create up to 100 handmade bottles per day, but he or she had to train for years to become that good. A machine in a factory could create 100 or more bottles an hour and be operated by workers who were much less skilled and were paid far less than a traditional glassblower.

Life in the United States changed forever during these years, as a more pastoral America yielded to a nation of factories, machines, and smokestacks. Workers in the new factories formed ever-stronger unions to protect themselves during the changing times of the Industrial Revolution.

The Creation of the Department of Labor

In 1903, the Department of Commerce and Labor was created both to support America's business interests and to protect its workers. It soon became clear, however, that the interests of business owners and those of their workers were often quite different and could not be fairly represented by one organization. The department tended to favor owners, who had all the money, power, and influence. Organized labor began to push for the creation of a separate and independent Department of Labor, and the U.S. Congress eventually agreed, presenting President William H. Taft with the Organic Act of the Department of Labor in 1913.

Taft was opposed to the bill that established the Department of Labor by dividing the previous U.S. Department of Commerce and Labor into two separate departments. He had recently lost the presidential election of 1912, and Woodrow Wilson was scheduled to become president in only a few hours. President Taft was pressured to sign the bill into law so that the new department would be established when President Wilson took over. President Wilson was a strong supporter of both the new department and the rights of workers. He appointed William Wilson as the first secretary of labor. Secretary Wilson, no relation to President Wilson, had many years of experience as the former secretary-treasurer of the United Mine Workers of America.

THE DEPARTMENT OF LABOR AT WORK: THE MINE SAFETY AND HEALTH ADMINISTRATION (MSHA)

The Mine Safety and Health Administration's Stay Out–Stay Alive program is a national public awareness campaign aimed at warning children and adults about the dangers of trespassing on active and abandoned mine sites. Every year, dozens of people are injured or killed in accidents on mine property. Each year, around Earth Day (April 22), representatives of Stay Out–Stay Alive visit schools, communities, and youth organizations throughout the country to educate children about the importance of staying away from working and abandoned mines. In addition, the MSHA operates Web sites geared toward miners that include information on mine accident and illness prevention.

In 1917, four years after the creation of the Department of Labor, the United States entered the First World War. During the war, the department was responsible for increasing productivity—especially in manufacturing—for the war effort. The department's War Labor Administration and War Labor Board, both administered by Secretary Wilson, oversaw working conditions for those laboring in wartime industries.

Woodrow Wilson had been an activist for labor before becoming president in 1913. Under his administration, the department was a strong advocate of workers' rights. When

Republican presidents Calvin Coolidge and Herbert Hoover were in office from 1920 to 1933, however, the DOL began to shift away from the interests of organized labor. Even so, during this time the department worked to protect children, migrant workers, and women through the creation of various labor bureaus.

The Depression and the New Deal

In 1929, the stock market experienced its greatest crash (or loss of value) in history, beginning a severe, decadelong economic depression known simply as the Great Depression. Many people lost all of their money in the stock market crash, banks closed, and by 1932, more than 25 percent of U.S. workers were unemployed—a total of more than 13 million people. President Hoover and his labor secretary, William Doak, did little to help workers during this deepening economic crisis.

The Depression lasted more than ten years. A far more active leader replaced Hoover as president in 1933—Franklin Delano Roosevelt (FDR). FDR took office, determined to pull America and its workers out of the Depression through his New Deal—a series of public projects and relief programs designed to put Americans back to work and protect their savings.

Thousands of Americans went hungry during this time, including many children who suffered long-term effects from

17

The Works Progress Administration (WPA) was one of the largest and best known of President Franklin D. Roosevelt's New Deal programs. It employed more than 8.5 million people at an average monthly salary of $41.57 to build bridges, roads, public buildings, public parks, and airports. The WPA also encouraged the endeavors of the nation's artists, musicians, and writers. Above, WPA workers lay a sidewalk in Perth Amboy, New Jersey, in 1938.

poor nutrition and no health care. Breadlines and soup kitchens became common sights in many American cities, with unemployed workers and their families waiting hours for a free cup of soup and a scrap of bread.

Roosevelt appointed Frances Perkins to be his secretary of labor. She was the first woman ever to serve as a secretary in any cabinet-level department. She and President Roosevelt worked so well together that she served from 1933 to 1945, throughout Roosevelt's entire four-term presidency.

Under Frances Perkins, the DOL took a major role in establishing the New Deal programs that helped the United

States overcome the Depression. One of the most important labor laws ever passed with the department's sponsorship was the Fair Labor Standards Act in 1938. It established the federal minimum wage at twenty-five cents an hour, and the eight-hour workday and forty-hour workweek, which we still have today.

The success of FDR's New Deal, along with the economic jumpstart provided by military manufacturing after America's 1941 entry into World War II, finally pulled the United States out of the Great Depression. During and after the war, unemployment rates fell and American industry began to boom. As the only major western nation to emerge from the war with a sound economy and an unharmed infrastructure, the United States soon found itself rebuilding much of Europe, friend and former foe alike. This activity further boosted the American economy.

In the 1950s, the United States was again a prosperous and productive nation. The economy was so healthy that workers were in demand and could ask employers for better pay and working conditions than they received during the Depression. With most of America's workers less vulnerable than they were in the 1930s, the DOL turned its attention to those who were still being left behind—migrant agricultural workers—and developed programs to protect this segment of American labor.

The DOL Changes with the Times

During President John F. Kennedy's administration in the early 1960s, the DOL was active in developing job training and safety programs. It also began to develop programs for cultural and social enrichment, especially for the growing populations of minority residents in the nation's inner cities. These social programs grew in the mid-1960s under President Lyndon B. Johnson's Great Society and War on Poverty initiatives. These programs were designed to combat poverty in America, partly through job training and other economic opportunities. Because steady, well-paying jobs are a key to eliminating poverty, the DOL became a leader in the "war," establishing the Manpower Administration, which trained and helped provide jobs for young urban workers and other groups of economically disadvantaged people.

During the administrations of Presidents Richard M. Nixon and Gerald R. Ford in the late 1960s and early 1970s, the DOL underwent important changes. The department was decentralized, which means that some of its duties were given to individual states to carry out. Yet the DOL continued to be an active force for job creation in the country. In 1969, the Job Corps was moved into the department, and the Comprehensive Employment and Training Administration (CETA) established training jobs under the control of local governments. The Emergency Employment Act provided

Filipino migrant workers harvest lettuce in a California field in 1939. California growers often preferred to hire Filipinos because they were seen as hard workers and quick learners and were willing to work for less money than Mexican and American migrant workers. Today, migrant agricultural laborers often continue to endure long hours, low pay, and poor working and living conditions.

more than 100,000 temporary jobs to struggling workers. In 1971, one of the most important offices of today's DOL was established—the Occupational Safety and Health Administration (OSHA), which sends inspectors into workplaces to ensure worker safety. During this time, the DOL also began to oversee private employer retirement plans in order to better protect workers' retirement savings. Unemployment insurance (UI) payments to those who were out of work were also increased in the early 1970s.

In the late 1970s, under President Jimmy Carter, the DOL improved its programs aimed at inner-city youth and the unemployed. The minimum wage was raised by more than $1 an hour to $3.35 an hour, covering farm workers for the first time. During this time, extreme inflation and an economic recession began.

Under President Ronald Reagan in the 1980s, the DOL's main goal was to stimulate an economy slowed down by a recession. Reagan felt the best way to do this was to eliminate many of the regulations placed upon American companies that are designed, among other things, to ensure worker safety, nondiscriminatory hiring practices, and fair wages. As a result, the department took charge of reducing and streamlining regulations, especially those covered by OSHA. Federal job programs were also cut, and the Job Training Partnership Act (JTPA) replaced CETA in 1983. Despite criticism from many labor groups and even some economists, during the 1980s many U.S. workers went back to work, inflation went down, and the economy greatly improved.

During the administrations of President Reagan and George H. W. Bush, three female secretaries of labor were appointed. Anne Dore McLaughlin, Elizabeth Dole, and Lynn Martin continued the tradition that President Roosevelt had established by appointing Frances Perkins as the country's first female cabinet secretary back in 1933.

When President William Jefferson Clinton took office in 1993, he appointed Robert Reich as his secretary of labor. Secretary Reich instituted the Retirement Protection Act, which strengthened employee pension plans and protected older workers. He also introduced the Family and Medical Leave Act of 1993, which guaranteed employees up to twelve weeks of unpaid leave for personal and medical reasons.

In 1997, Alexis Herman became the secretary of labor, after serving as the head of the DOL's Women's Bureau. Under Secretary Herman, the department established more programs to help women and minorities, and programs to lead people away from welfare programs and back to work.

In 2001, President George W. Bush appointed Elaine Chao, the former president of the national United Way and director of the Peace Corps, to take the leadership of the DOL. The first Asian American woman ever to serve in a cabinet-level position, Secretary Chao developed programs to help workers in the United States adjust to the new technology-driven economy, including the Twenty-first Century Workforce Initiative.

As Secretary Chao's efforts indicate, the DOL is poised for the future and, as it has since its inception in 1913, continues to grow and change with the times.

CHAPTER TWO

The Secretaries of Labor

One unique aspect of the Department of Labor is that of all of the federal cabinet offices, the DOL has had the greatest number of female secretaries. President Franklin D. Roosevelt established this tradition in 1933 when he appointed Frances Perkins as the first female secretary of labor. Secretary Perkins was also the first female secretary of any cabinet department.

All of the secretaries of labor have been dedicated to the welfare of American workers, but some of the ones we discuss here were very involved in labor-related causes even before their appointments. William Wilson, the nation's first secretary of labor, was one such secretary, establishing the DOL as a champion of workers' rights from the very beginning.

William B. Wilson (1913–1921)

Before William Wilson became the secretary of labor, he was the secretary-treasurer of the United Mine Workers of America. As secretary of labor, Wilson helped shape American working conditions of the twentieth century by advocating eight-hour workdays, strong unions, workers' compensation (money paid to employees after workplace injuries and accidents), child labor laws, and workplace safety.

Nearly all of the programs that the Department of Labor still conducts today were first established by Secretary Wilson. When he took charge of the DOL, the department had 2,000 employees and four bureaus, all left over from the former Department of Commerce and Labor. The four bureaus were Children, Immigration and Naturalization, Labor Statistics, and a Division of Conciliation (designed to forge agreements between workers and owners or managers). During the First World War (1914–1918), Secretary Wilson made the department a key part of President Woodrow Wilson's administration by coordinating the transfer of 6 million U.S. workers to essential war industries. After the war, the DOL helped move them back to their former jobs. Secretary Wilson also established programs designed to encourage the employment of women, the retraining of veterans with disabilities, fair employment for minorities, and good labor-management relations.

Born in 1862 in Scotland, Wilson immigrated to the United States at age eight. His family was evicted from its home in Scotland after a coal-mining strike, and settled in the small mining town of Arnot, Pennsylvania. Later, Wilson raised his own family of eleven children on a farm in the nearby town of Blossburg, Pennsylvania. After becoming a union activist, Wilson was blacklisted from working due to his pro-union activities. These early experiences of hardship and poor treatment at the hands of mine owners no doubt resulted in Secretary Wilson's unique interest in the concerns of miners. Yet as secretary of labor, he fought effectively for the well-being of all American workers.

Frances Perkins (1933–1945)

The first female secretary of labor, Frances Perkins, was also the longest-serving secretary. Her close and productive working relationship with President Franklin D. Roosevelt began with her appointment to serve as his industrial commissioner when he was governor of New York. This led to her appointment as secretary of labor when Roosevelt became president in 1933.

Born in 1882 in Boston, Massachusetts, Perkins graduated from Mount Holyoke College in 1902, and was trained as a social worker. Secretary Perkins was active in Progressive social causes her entire life. Progressives were people who felt that social improvement could come through government action.

Frances Perkins *(third from right)* stands behind President Franklin D. Roosevelt as he signs the Social Security bill into law in 1935. As a Depression-era secretary of labor—and the first female cabinet secretary—Perkins played a key role in the design and implementation of New Deal legislation, including minimum wage laws and the Social Security Act.

She began her involvement in labor with her investigation of the Triangle Shirtwaist Fire in 1911. This was the worst factory fire in New York City's history. Within fifteen minutes of it breaking out, the fire killed 146 people, mostly women. The fire and the deaths were eventually found to have largely been a result of poor working conditions.

During her twelve years as secretary, Frances Perkins helped develop nearly all of the labor programs and legislation of Roosevelt's New Deal administration. "I came to Washington to work for God, FDR, and the millions of forgotten, plain common workingmen," Perkins said (as quoted by the Department of Labor Web site). As chair of the president's Council on Economic Security, she led the hearings that established the Social Security Act of 1935, providing payments and much-needed financial support to America's retired workers.

After she stepped down as secretary of labor in 1945, she was asked by FDR's successor, President Harry S. Truman, to serve on the U.S. Civil Service Commission, which she did until 1952, when her husband died. Following her government service career, Frances Perkins continued to be active as a teacher and lecturer until her death in 1965.

Arthur J. Goldberg (1961–1962)

In 1961, President John F. Kennedy appointed Arthur J. Goldberg, the son of Ukrainian immigrants, to serve as secretary of labor. Arthur Goldberg was born on August 8, 1908, in a tough, blue-collar neighborhood on the west side of Chicago. Goldberg was the youngest of eleven children and the only one of his siblings to graduate from high school or college. His father, Joseph, was a well-educated Jewish immigrant from Kiev, a Ukrainian city known for its persecution of Jewish families. Once in the United States, Joseph Goldberg could only find employment as a peddler or fruit seller despite his education.

Because of his early background in a poor Chicago neighborhood and his father's strong work ethic and difficult struggle to

Arthur J. Goldberg *(right)* was inspired to join the army following the Japanese attack on Pearl Harbor in December 1941. He served as special assistant within the Office of Strategic Services (OSS), an intelligence organization that would evolve into the CIA. He was assigned to the OSS's labor division, where he helped support the underground anti-Fascist activities of European union leaders struggling against the domination of the Axis powers of Germany and Italy.

support his family, Arthur Goldberg grew up with a sympathy for and understanding of ordinary workers. Inspired by the examples of success presented by Jewish Supreme Court justices Louis Brandeis and Benjamin Cardozo, Goldberg received a scholarship to Crane Junior College. He later transferred to Northwestern University, earning his bachelor's degree when he was only nineteen. By the time he was twenty-one, he had completed his law degree at Northwestern University's law school, all while working in construction to pay tuition.

During the New Deal years of President Roosevelt's administration, Goldberg worked with labor-related court cases through his private practice, strongly opposing the American Bar Association's negative opinions about FDR's many programs designed to benefit unemployed workers. During the Second World War (1939–1945), the Japanese attack on Pearl Harbor as well as Nazi Germany's persecution of European Jews motivated Goldberg to serve his country in the most direct way possible— he joined the armed forces. Although he was not able to serve in the U.S. Marine Corps as he wished, he became a commissioned major in the army, serving with General "Wild Bill" Donovan and conducting many undercover operations for the Office of Strategic Services (OSS), the military intelligence agency that later became the Central Intelligence Agency (CIA).

After the war, Goldberg played an important part in the development of modern organized labor. He was a leading figure in the merger of the American Federation of Labor (AFL) and Congress of Industrial Organizations (CIO), the two leading trade unions in the nation. Today, the massive and influential labor union is known as the AFL-CIO.

Appointed as President Kennedy's secretary of labor in 1961, Goldberg became a leader in fighting job discrimination by developing the Equal Employment Opportunity Act, which forbids hiring decisions based on an applicant's race, sex, religion, or ethnicity. He was a leader in Kennedy's New Frontier programs, which were meant to fight poverty and prejudice. Goldberg's time as secretary of labor was short, however. When Supreme Court justice Felix Frankfurter retired in 1962, President Kennedy appointed Goldberg to replace him. Goldberg served from 1962 to 1965 as a Supreme Court justice.

Elizabeth Dole (1989–1990)

Before becoming one of North Carolina's representatives in the U.S. Senate, Elizabeth Dole (wife of retired senator Robert Dole) was an effective secretary of labor under President George H. W. Bush. In her brief but busy time in office, she helped raise the minimum wage for regular workers and youth trainees, and developed more labor programs for women and minorities.

Elizabeth Dole was born in 1936 in Salisbury, North Carolina. She graduated from Duke University in 1958, then went on to Harvard University, where she received a master's degree in 1960 and her JD (Juris Doctor, a law degree) from Harvard Law School in 1965. She moved to Washington, D.C., in 1966, first working on issues related to handicapped people. Even though she was a political independent at the time, Republican president Richard Nixon appointed her to a seven-year term on the Federal Trade Commission (FTC) in 1973. Dole also served as President Nixon's director of the Committee on Consumer Interests, making sure that products were safe and did not make any misleading claims in their advertising.

The Americans with Disabilities Act, which went into effect in 1992, forbids employers, government agencies, and labor unions from discriminating against qualified workers who are disabled. It also forces employers and businesses to accommodate disabled workers by, for example, purchasing office equipment designed for disabled workers, such as this computer keyboard that can be used with one hand.

President Ronald Reagan appointed Dole as secretary of transportation in 1983, a job she held for four years. Then, President George H. W. Bush appointed her as secretary of labor in 1989. Her greatest achievement in office was the passage of the Americans with Disabilities Act, which forbids private employers, state and local governments, employment agencies, and labor unions from discriminating against qualified individuals with disabilities. All decisions related to job application procedures, hiring, firing, promotion, and pay must be made without regard to the disability. As secretary, Dole also worked to increase safety and health in the workplace and advocated upgrading the skills of the American workforce. She played a key role in resolving the eleven-month Pittston Coal Strike in southwest Virginia.

Dole resigned as secretary of labor in 1990 to become president of the American Red Cross, representing that

THE DEPARTMENT OF LABOR AT WORK: THE VETERANS' EMPLOYMENT AND TRAINING SERVICE (VETS)

The VETS' Disabled Veterans' Outreach Program (DVOP) is designed to develop job and training opportunities for veterans, especially those veterans who have become disabled due to military service. DVOP specialists provide outreach and offer assistance to disabled and other veterans by promoting community and employer support for employment and training opportunities, including apprenticeships and on-the-job training.

DVOP specialists work with employers, veterans' organizations, the Departments of Veterans' Affairs and Defense, and community-based organizations to place veterans in appropriate jobs and training programs.

organization nationally and internationally from 1991 to 2000. In 1999, Dole unsuccessfully sought the Republican presidential nomination but in 2002 won a Senate seat as a representative of North Carolina.

Elaine L. Chao (2001–)

The secretary of labor under President George W. Bush was the first Asian American woman appointed to any cabinet-level position, as well as the first Chinese American to be appointed to the cabinet. Elaine Chao was born in 1953 in Taipei, Taiwan, the daughter of James Chao, a Shanghai businessman, and Ruth Mu-lan Chao, a historian. Elaine Chao immigrated to the United States at age eight, eventually studying economics at Mount Holyoke University and then graduating from Harvard School of Business with an MBA degree (Master of Business Administration).

First working as an investment banker for Citicorp, Chao soon became involved with political and charitable causes. She was selected as a White House fellow in 1983 and began working in the Office of Policy Development. In 1986, she became the deputy administrator and then the chairperson of the U.S. Maritime Commission. President George H. W. Bush nominated her as the deputy secretary of transportation in 1989. From 1991 to 1992, Chao served as director of the Peace Corps.

Chao resigned from that position to take the difficult job of president of the national United Way in 1992. Before her appointment, the United Way charity had experienced a major financial and management scandal, and she was charged with fixing the group's finances and restoring its good reputation. Chao was able to renew trust and confidence in the organization during her four-year tenure as president.

Beginning in 1996, Chao served as a fellow of the Heritage Foundation, a research and educational institute devoted to developing and promoting conservative public

Elaine L. Chao, the twenty-fourth secretary of labor *(right)*, stands with Secretary of Defense Donald H. Rumsfeld *(left)* to announce a new Department of Labor initiative designed to ease reentry into the civilian workforce by members of the military. The plan would expand America's Job Bank to include recruiting for military jobs, and employers would be encouraged to hire returning reservists and military spouses.

policies. In 2001, President George W. Bush appointed her as secretary of labor. Following his reelection in 2004, Chao remained as Secretary of Labor in Bush's second presidential administration. In this position, Chao is especially sensitive to the concerns of women and immigrants in the workforce. She has also confronted the challenges posed to American workers by the new global technological economy by launching the Twenty-first Century Workforce Initiative. This program attempts to ensure that all American workers make the transition from a more industrial economy to a more computer-and technology-driven workplace and find fulfilling and well-paying careers in the process.

CHAPTER THREE

How the Department of Labor Works

When Secretary William Wilson took over the newly independent Department of Labor in 1913, he found four bureaus and 2,000 employees left over from the combined Department of Commerce and Labor. Today, the office of the secretary of labor oversees tens of thousands of employees working in more than twenty bureaus, offices, and administrations, each responsible for various aspects of the modern workforce.

Some of the DOL's most important work takes place in the following eight department agencies:

Occupational Safety and Health Administration (OSHA)

OSHA is committed to protecting the lives and health of American workers by ensuring good workplace conditions and preventing on-the-job accidents. Working with state-level agencies that share similar responsibilities, OSHA and its partners send out about 2,100 inspectors from more than 200 offices throughout the country to inspect workplaces, investigate complaints, and enforce OSHA's workplace safety and health standards. Nearly every working man and woman in the nation comes under OSHA's jurisdiction.

Employee Benefits Security Administration (EBSA)

The EBSA is responsible for assisting America's workers in obtaining and maintaining their employee benefits, including pensions and health plans.

Bureau of Labor Statistics (BLS)

The BLS is the federal government's main compiler of labor statistics. The data it collects—such as unemployment rates or job growth statistics—allows the government to chart the nation's social and economic health and the well-being of its workers and workplaces. The data collected by the BLS is shared with the Department of Labor, other federal and state agencies, the U.S. Congress, business and labor groups, and the American public.

THE DEPARTMENT OF LABOR AT WORK: THE OCCUPATIONAL HEALTH AND SAFETY ADMINISTRATION (OSHA)

An OSHA technician prepares workplace air samples for testing.

OSHA is charged with inspecting American businesses, identifying unsafe or unhealthy workplace conditions, and suggesting penalties for those businesses that are not in compliance with OSHA standards. In order to avoid penalties and fines, businesses can call upon a free consulting service funded by OSHA. Employers who use the service are visited by consultants who identify hazards in the workplace, suggest general approaches to solving a safety or health problem, provide a written report summarizing their findings, and assist the employer in developing an effective safety and health program. The consultants do not penalize the employer for any safety or health infractions, nor do they share their findings with OSHA. By calling in consultants before an OSHA inspection, an employer can avoid large fines or even the threat of being shut down.

Employment and Training Administration (ETA)

The ETA provides grants and programs to help workers train for and get jobs, including programs such as Job Corps and grants to states that provide programs like One-Stop Career Centers. Many people are not aware that several of the Department of Labor's programs are conducted in cooperation with state employment departments and are funded by both state and federal governments. Still other training programs are conducted by private organizations that contract with the Department of Labor, such as Goodwill Industries, an organization that provides training and employment for disabled or long-term unemployed people.

Office of Disability Employment Policy (ODEP)

Created in 2001, the ODEP works to increase employment opportunities for adults and youths with disabilities. It does this by expanding disabled workers' access to training, education, and employment supports. It also helps disabled entrepreneurs who want to go into business for themselves. In addition, the ODEP educates employers and state and local agencies on the benefits of hiring people with disabilities and how to accommodate disabled employees in the workplace.

Women's Bureau (WB)

One of the original bureaus established in the early days of the Labor Department, the Women's Bureau is currently focused on

A female firefighter holds a fire axe as she climbs a ladder during a drill in San Diego, California. San Diego has taken the lead in the nation's efforts to offer equal opportunities to women wishing to enter fire companies. As of 2003, the San Diego Fire Department had 38 female firefighter paramedics among its 800 firefighters, and the California Department of Forestry and Fire Protection had 47 women in its corps of 196 firefighters.

strengthening American families by increasing the financial security and job flexibility of working mothers. The bureau is committed to promoting well-paying job opportunities for women, as well as working to improve the skills of female job seekers. In addition, the WB seeks to improve the working conditions women face and encourage employers to fairly consider female applicants for jobs such as firefighters, mechanics, and construction workers, which were traditionally done by males.

Today, more than 100 million people are employed full-time in the United States, and 43.7 percent of them are women, according to a 2002 survey by the Women's Bureau. By 2010, women are expected to represent 48 percent of the workforce. The top twenty occupations for women are still dominated by jobs traditionally filled by female workers—retail salespeople and cashiers, secretaries, elementary school teachers, nurses, and nurses' aides. Overall, salaries for all of the top twenty occupations for women nationwide are about 22 percent less than the salaries earned by men in the same or similar job categories. Achieving salary equality between men and women working in the same profession is an important goal of the WB and the Department of Labor. Progress has been made over the decades (in 1950, women earned only about 50 percent of what their male counterparts took home), yet a large earning gap remains to be closed.

Employment Standards Administration (ESA)

The ESA is the largest agency within the U.S. Department of Labor. It is charged with enforcing and administering the nation's laws governing wages and working conditions. This includes laws concerning child labor, minimum wages, overtime, family and medical leave, equal employment opportunity in businesses with federal contracts and subcontracts, and workers' compensation for employees injured on the job.

The ESA is made up of four main programs—the Office of Federal Contract Compliance Programs, the Office of Labor-Management Standards, the Office of Workers' Compensation

41

Programs, and the Wage and Hour Division. The Office of Federal Contract Compliance Programs ensures that private companies that do business with the federal government comply with its equal opportunity and nondiscrimination hiring laws. The Office of Labor-Management Standards seeks to promote democratic systems within unions and protect the rights of union members. Workers who are injured on the job are protected by the Office of Workers' Compensation Programs, which makes payments to help cover employees' medical expenses and lost wages. The enforcement of federal laws concerning minimum wage, overtime pay, child labor, family and medical leave, and the rights of migrant agricultural laborers is the duty of the Wage and Hour Division.

Unemployment Insurance (UI)

Through a federal-state partnership established by the Social Security Act (SSA) and Federal Unemployment Tax Act (FUTA), each state receives funds from the federal government that provide temporary financial assistance to workers who are unemployed through no fault of their own (for example, someone who was laid off rather than someone who quit or was fired). Unemployment insurance is provided through state employment agencies and funded by deductions (a sort of tax) from employers. In order to receive it, unemployed workers must usually file a claim every week. As part of this claim, applicants must report any money earned that week and any job offers received. They must also show that they have been actively seeking new employment.

In a nation of 10 million employers, 125 million full- and part-time workers, and the families who depend upon them, the programs and policies of the Department of Labor affect the lives of everyone in America. Ensuring safer workplaces, providing financial help following layoffs, and fighting for the rights of female and minority job applicants are just a few of the many different duties the Department of Labor undertakes to protect American workers and create fair and safe workplaces. Without the energetic efforts of this department, American workers would be at the mercy of unregulated employers who could demand long hours spent in dangerous conditions for very little pay. The Department of Labor's work on behalf of American workers illustrates the great value and necessity of government involvement in public policy.

CHAPTER FOUR

The Department of Labor in the Twenty-first Century

President George W. Bush's secretary of labor, Elaine Chao, described her vision for America's twenty-first century workforce as "one in which everyone can participate . . . where jobs and opportunities are available for those leaving welfare, job training is accessible for those left behind, disability never bars a qualified person from the workplace, and where parents have an easier time balancing the responsibilities of work and home."

The overall goals of the DOL at the beginning of the twenty-first century are simple and straightforward and have changed little in the more than ninety years since the DOL's creation. They include:

- The creation of more jobs
- The protection of workers' health and safety
- The enforcement of existing labor laws
- Greater opportunity for the disabled
- Improved worker training and education
- Preparing Americans for the workplace demands of the future

New Twists on Old Problems

While the DOL is planning for a future economy and workforce that will be highly educated, technologically sophisticated, and global in nature, problems of the past—including poor working conditions and employer exploitation of workers—persist. While some employees are now able to "telecommute"—work at home via computers linked up with a main office—other workers still labor in dangerous and unhealthy working conditions reminiscent of early twentieth-century sweatshops.

A sweatshop is a factory that manufactures simple goods (such as clothing or shoes) and pays its workers very little, often far less than minimum wage. Workers must endure extremely uncomfortable and unsafe conditions. The DOL was created in part to combat the shocking working conditions in these businesses first brought to the public's attention by the Triangle Shirtwaist Fire of 1911. Far from

Unfortunately, sweatshops are not a thing of the past. Segments of the garment industry continue to employ workers—often recent or illegal immigrants—at below minimum wage. They often labor in unsafe and uncomfortable conditions for far longer than the standard eight-hour shift. Above, a worker sews garments in New York City. New York and Los Angeles are the country's main garment hubs. Sweatshop Watch, a California organization, believes that over 60 percent of garment factories, in both cities, violate minimum wage and overtime laws.

having won this war, the DOL continues to combat the often illegal practices of these factories. Today, many American clothing manufacturers farm out their work to sweatshops that employ recent or illegal immigrants, or are based overseas and rely on cheap foreign labor.

Sweatshops keep attracting workers in desperate need of employment. Studies conducted by the DOL from 1997 to 2000 found that 67 percent of Los Angeles garment factories and 63 percent of New York garment factories violate minimum

On March 25, 1911, a fire broke out in the Triangle Shirtwaist Factory, where 500 women, mostly Jewish immigrants between the ages of thirteen and twenty-three, cut fabric and sewed garments. Locked doors designed to keep the workers at their sewing machines prevented their escape, resulting in the deaths of 146 workers in less than fifteen minutes. Many of them jumped from the building's ninth floor.

wage and overtime laws. Ninety-eight percent of Los Angeles garment factories have workplace health and safety problems serious enough to lead to severe injuries or death. The DOL and state labor agencies fight to improve conditions in these sweatshops, but they are often made aware of problems only after it is too late to avert tragedy. In 1991, twenty-five workers died in a fire at a poultry processing plant in Hamlet, North Carolina. The workers were trapped behind illegally locked doors. In 1995, a clothing manufacturer in El Monte, California, was discovered to be paying Southeast Asian immigrants pennies to make garments for sale in U.S. department stores.

Other longstanding DOL concerns, such as worker injury and child labor, also continue to be addressed by the department in the twenty-first century, though the problems are slightly different. For example, where the DOL once tried to prevent gruesome industrial accidents involving heavy machinery, it now is combating "repetitive motion injuries," or the types of injuries that occur from working many hours a day at computer keyboards. When a worker's hand or wrist makes the same motion hundreds of times a day—such as clicking a mouse—the bones and muscles are placed under great stress, and serious pain and injury can result. Specially designed chairs and desks along with sufficient breaks from constant typing can prevent these injuries, and the DOL tries to get this information out to employers.

While in most cases younger children are no longer allowed to hold jobs, teenagers do make up a large portion of the part-time workforce. The DOL is committed to ensuring that they receive fair pay, are in safe working environments, and, in the case of fourteen- and fifteen-year-olds, will not be asked to work more than twenty hours a week while they are still attending school. DOL offices across the country, such as the One-Stop Career Centers, help teens and young workers select, prepare for, and begin careers that fit their talents and interests. An "investment in the future" will also continue to be made through the Workforce Investment Act, which provides job training for youths ages eighteen and under, preparing

THE DEPARTMENT OF LABOR AT WORK: WOMEN'S ENTREPRENEURSHIP IN THE TWENTY-FIRST CENTURY

During Elaine L. Chao's first two years as secretary of labor, she sponsored a series of conferences focusing on the needs of today's women entrepreneurs, including solving the persistent problems that prevent the growth and long-term financial health of businesses owned by women. These conferences have been held in Connecticut, Pennsylvania, Florida, Ohio, and Washington, D.C. In addition, the DOL's Women's Bureau encourages the mentoring of female business owners by successful female executives and offers a training program to disabled women who wish to become entrepreneurs. Through the Occupational Safety and Health Administration, the DOL offers consultation and advice to small business owners, many of whom are women.

them to transition smoothly into jobs that pay well and are in high demand.

The Importance of Education

Of all the labor issues that the DOL will confront in the future, education is the most crucial. John Chambers, the CEO of Cisco Systems, a high-tech computer company that started with two owners in the late 1980s and now employs more than 34,000 people worldwide, was one of the business leaders and employers involved in the Twenty-first Century Workforce Initiative. "Education is one of the most vital tools for our current and future workforce," Chambers said in an article entitled "Jobs Will Go to the Best Educated Workforce." "I often say that education and the Internet are the two equalizers in life."

The high-tech jobs of the future will demand more education and training than ever before. Chambers and other business leaders believe that wherever the most educated workforce is located, jobs and companies will follow. Highly educated workers could be in California or Massachusetts or Georgia, but they could also be in Seoul, Singapore, London, or Paris. If the American workforce cannot keep up with the latest technology, business will flow elsewhere and the economy will suffer. The Department of Labor is working to develop programs that will educate and train U.S. workers to compete not just locally or nationally, but in the international job market as well.

Tools like "e-learning," or online education, could help improve the knowledge and skill levels of American workers. Although the DOL has little influence over the education system, the quality of America's schools and the students they produce eventually affect the quality of jobs and employment. The American university system is the best in the world, and the large number of international students who come to the United States to study confirms its excellent reputation.

Machine shop department head Joe Guliotti *(third from left)* instructs his students on how to operate a plastic injection molding machine at the Regional Vocational Technical School in Ansonia, Connecticut. Vocational technical schools usually serve full-time high school students and part-time adult students. High school students generally receive a high school diploma as well as a certificate in a particular occupation. Adult students are provided apprentice training and programs for upgrading their skills.

According to the Twenty-first Century Workforce Initiative, however, there are concerns about the K–12 education system. In 2002, the nation's eighth-grade students scored eighteenth and nineteenth in math and science against other countries worldwide. This poor performance may eventually affect the willingness of both American and international companies to seek graduates from American schools for employment, especially in high-tech industries.

In order to help combat this trend and improve the education and competitiveness of American workers, the DOL will offer high-tech job training programs. It will also increase its cooperation with high schools, vocational schools, community colleges, and four-year colleges and universities.

Protecting Retired Workers

The DOL is also planning to strengthen programs that improve workers' financial well-being when they retire. People are living longer than ever before, and this trend is expected to increase in the twenty-first century. Where workers of the first half of the twentieth century might have lived for only a few years after their retirement, today's employees can expect to need income for twenty or more years beyond their retirements at age sixty-five. Social security payments do not pay enough money to retirees to provide them with a good standard of living or the funds necessary to pay for medical bills and unexpected illnesses. As a result, the DOL is committed to improving retirement programs and ensuring the financial health of current retirement funds long into the future. The department is placing a special emphasis on programs that help retired women because a disproportionate number of people living in poverty are women, particularly senior citizens.

As declared in the Twenty-first Century Workforce Initiative mission statement, the DOL is committed to making sure that no worker—whether male, female, old, young, disabled, or a recent immigrant—gets left behind in the nation's march toward security and prosperity.

Conclusion

Jobs of the future are projected to grow in many areas, especially the health care industry and many different service industry and professional jobs. The Department of Labor is working to establish links between the companies in these fields and local education and training providers in order to create workers ready and able to fill these new positions. By attempting to identify in this way where workers are needed and where they are not, the DOL hopes that job shortages and industry crises can be avoided in the future, ensuring a highly trained, well-paid, and stable twenty-first–century workforce.

Many people are not aware that nearly all labor and business experts worldwide acknowledge that the great economic strength

Donna Roberson, a maintenance mechanic at the John Deere Harvester Works in East Moline, Illinois, stands atop a Women in Industry float during the East Moline Labor Day Parade on September 1, 2003. First celebrated on September 5, 1882, in New York City, Labor Day honors the energy, spirit, and industry of the millions of workers who continue to make the United States one of the most prosperous and productive nations in the world.

and worldwide influence of the United States comes from its workforce. By protecting the health and safety of American workers and encouraging a high quality of education and training, the DOL has helped create the conditions necessary for a stable, content, energetic, and creative workforce, one that has catapulted its country to the forefront of the world's economic powers.

As the nation confronts the new challenges and uncertainties of the twenty-first century, one thing is certain: as long as there are jobs available and people able to perform them, the Department of Labor will be there to ensure the safety, fair treatment, and productivity of the American workforce.

TIMELINE

August 14, 1935	The Social Security Act is passed, and the Unemployment Insurance system is created.
June 25, 1938	The Fair Labor Standards Act is passed, establishing the eight-hour workday and the forty-hour workweek.
1945–1948	Lewis B. Schwellenbach
1948–1953	Maurice J. Tobin
1953	Martin P. Durkin
1953–1961	James P. Mitchell
1961–1962	Arthur J. Goldberg
March 15, 1962	The Manpower Development and Training Act is passed, allowing for the training and retraining of thousands of workers unemployed due to automation and technological change.
1962–1969	W. Willard Wirtz
June 10, 1963	The Equal Pay Act is passed, which fights gender discrimination by providing for the equal payment of men and women for equal or similar work.
August 20, 1964	The Economic Opportunity Act is passed, creating the Job Corps.
December 15, 1967	The Age Discrimination Act is passed, prohibiting discrimination on the basis of age in job application procedures, hiring, firing, or promotion.
1969–1970	George P. Shultz
1970–1973	James D. Hodgson
April 28, 1971	The Occupational Safety and Health Administration is established, designed to ensure safe and healthy workplaces in America.
1973–1975	Peter J. Brennan

1975–1976	John T. Dunlop
1976–1977	W. J. Usery Jr.
1977–1981	Ray Marshall
1981–1985	Raymond J. Donovan
January 14, 1983	The Migrant and Seasonal Agricultural Worker Protection Act is passed.
1985–1987	William E. Brock
1987–1989	Ann Dore McLaughlin
1989–1990	Elizabeth Hanford Dole
July 26, 1990	The Americans with Disabilities Act is passed.
1991–1993	Lynn Morley Martin
1993–1997	Robert B. Reich
February 5, 1993	The Family and Medical Leave Act is passed, granting eligible employees up to twelve weeks of unpaid leave following the birth or adoption of a child; to care for a relative with a serious health condition; or because of the employee's own serious health condition.
1997–2001	Alexis M. Herman
2001–	Elaine L. Chao
September 11, 2001	The DOL orders a massive mobilization of disaster relief aid to the economic victims of the 9/11 attacks on New York City and the Pentagon in Arlington, Virginia.
April 23, 2004	The DOL issues new regulations for expanding the number of workers eligible for overtime pay.

GLOSSARY

bill A draft of a law presented to a legislature and submitted to a vote.

cabinet A council of the chief advisers of a head of state.

cabinet-level department A government office headed by a key adviser to a head of state, such as the president of the United States.

economy The flow of money within a country, state, region, city, town, or household.

federal Relating to the central governing authority in a nation made up of several states or territories.

legislation Proposed rules created by a decision-making body, such as the U.S. Congress or a town council.

manufacturing Making products by hand or machine from raw materials.

pension Regular payments made to a retiree by the government or his or her former employer.

productivity The quality of being able to perform a large amount of good work in a short period of time.

prosperity The condition of being successful and well-off.

statistics Information that is collected, counted, analyzed, and presented publicly; information that is collected to increase the understanding of a certain issue.

sweatshop A factory in which employees work for long hours and little pay, usually in dangerous, unhealthy, or uncomfortable conditions.

union A confederation, or alliance, of independent individuals with a common purpose.

**U.S. Bureau of Labor
  Statistics (BLS)**
Postal Square Building
2 Massachusetts Avenue NE
Washington, DC 20212-0001
(202) 691-5200
Web site: http://www.bls.gov

U.S. Department of Labor
Frances Perkins Building
200 Constitution Avenue NW
Washington, DC 20210
(866) 4-USA-DOL (487-2365)
Web site: http://www.dol.gov

Wirtz Labor Library
U.S. Department of Labor
Frances Perkins Building
Room N2445
200 Constitution Avenue NW
Washington, DC 20210

Web site: http://www.dol.gov/
  oasam/library/main.htm

Women's Bureau (WB)
U.S. Department of Labor
200 Constitution Avenue NW
Room S-3002
Washington, DC 20210
(800) 827-5335 or (202) 693-6710
Web site: http://www.dol.gov/wb

WEB SITES
Due to the changing nature of
Internet links, the Rosen Publishing
Group, Inc., has developed an
online list of Web sites related to
the subject of this book. This site
is updated regularly. Please use this
link to access the list:

www.rosenlinks.com/tyg/labo

FOR FURTHER READING

Broyles, Janell. *The Triangle Shirtwaist Factory Fire of 1911*. New York, NY: The Rosen Publishing Group, Inc., 2004.

Colman, Penny. *Mother Jones and the March of the Mill Children*. Brookfield, CT: Millbrook Press, 1994.

Colman, Penny. *Strike!: The Bitter Struggle of American Workers from Colonial Times to the Present*. Brookfield, CT: Millbrook Press, 1995.

Gourley, Catherine. *Good Girl Work: Factories, Sweatshops, and How Women Changed Their Role in the American Workforce*. Brookfield, CT: Millbrook Press, 1999.

Josephson, Judith Pinkerton. *Mother Jones: Fierce Fighter for Workers' Rights*. Minneapolis, MN: Lerner Publications Co., 1996.

Stein, R. Conrad. *The Pullman Strike and the Labor Movement in American History*. Berkeley Heights, NJ: Enslow Publishers, Inc., 2001.

Woog, Adam. *A Sweatshop During the Industrial Revolution*. San Diego, CA: Lucent Books, 2002.

BIBLIOGRAPHY

Boal, Mark. "An American Sweatshop." Mother Jones Magazine Online. August 19, 1999. Retrieved September 2003 (http://www.mother-jones.com/mother_jones/MJ99/boal.html).

Chambers, John T. "Jobs Will Go to the Best Educated Workforce." Cisco Systems. October 2002. Retrieved May 2004 (http://newsroom.cisco.com/dlls/tln/exec_team/chambers/pdf/article10_2002.pdf).

City of Blossburg, Pennsylvania. "William Beauchop Wilson: Secretary of Labor." September 2002. Retrieved September 2003 (http://www.blossburg.org/wb_wilson/thestory_6.htm).

Colman, Penny. *A Woman Unafraid: The Achievements of Frances Perkins*. New York, NY: Atheneum, 1993.

Department of Labor. "Frances Perkins (1880–1965): 1989 Labor Hall of Fame Honoree." Retrieved May 2004 (http://www.dol.gov/oasam/programs/laborhall/fp.htm).

Facts on File. "Issues and Controversies: Labor Unions." August 2002. Retrieved September 2003 (http://www.2facts.com/ICOF/temp/61867tempi0202070.asp#i0202070_1).

Gorn, Elliott J. *Mother Jones: The Most Dangerous Woman in America*. New York, NY: Hill & Wang, 2002.

Hickey, Jennifer G. "Chao Labors to Help U.S. Workforce." *Insight Magazine*, July 2, 2001, pp. 36–39.

Kessler-Harris, Alice. *Out to Work: A History of Wage-Earning Women in the United States*. New York, NY: Oxford University Press, 2003.

Kheel Center for Labor-Management Documentation and Archives. "The Triangle Shirtwaist Fire." Cornell University. Retrieved September 2003 (http://www.ilr.cornell.edu/trianglefire/narrative3.html).

Laughlin, Kathleen A. *Women's Work and Public Policy: A History of the Women's Bureau, U.S. Department of Labor, 1945–1970.* Tempe, AZ: Medieval and Renaissance Texts and Studies, 2000.

Lichtenstein, Nelson. *State of the Union: A Century of American Labor.* Princeton, NJ: Princeton University Press, 2003.

Mother Jones. "The March of the Mill Children." Chapter X in *Autobiography of Mother Jones.* Retrieved September 2003 (http://womenshistory.about.com/library/etext/mj/bl_mj10.htm).

Murray, R. Emmett, and Thomas Geoghegan. *Lexicon of Labor: More Than 500 Key Terms, Biographical Sketches, and Historical Insights Concerning Labor in America.* New York, NY: New Press, 1998.

Shils, Edward B. "Arthur Goldberg: Proof of the American Dream." *Monthly Labor Review,* January 1997. Retrieved September 2003 (http://www.bls.gov/opub/mlr/1997/01/art5full.pdf).

Striegel, Lawrence. "Mother Jones' Crusade." Newsday. 2003. Retrieved September 2003 (http://www.newsday.com/news/education/sbp/ny-sbp_62503,0,3791838.story?coll=ny-sbp-headlines).

Triece, Mary E. *Protest and Popular Culture: Women in the U.S.A. Labor Movement.* Boulder, CO: Westview Press, 2000.

U.S. Social Security Administration. "Social Security Pioneers: Frances Perkins." Retrieved September 2003 (http://www.ssa.gov/history/fperkins.html).

Von Drehle, David. *Triangle: The Fire That Changed America.* New York, NY: Atlantic Monthly Press, 2003.

Zieger, Robert H. *American Workers, American Unions.* Baltimore, MD: Johns Hopkins University Press, 1994.

INDEX

ABOUT THE AUTHOR

Amy Sterling Casil is an award-winning author who has written several books on technology, American history, government, and public policy.

PHOTO CREDITS

Front cover (top and portraits) The United States Department of Labor; front and back covers (bottom), pp. 6–7 © Industry and Technology/DigitalVision; back cover (top), pp. 3, 4 (circle) © Business and Occupations/PhotoDisc; pp. 4–5 © Conceptual Still Life/Digital Stock; pp. 10, 27 © Library of Congress Prints and Photographs Division; pp. 14, 18 © AP/Wide World Photos; p. 21 © Corbis; p. 29 © Hulton Archive/Getty Images; p. 32 © Owen Franken/Corbis; p. 35 Helene C. Stikkel, The United States Department of Defense; p. 38 Shawn Moore/OSHA News Photo; p. 40 © Gilles Mingasson/Liaison/Getty Images; p. 46 © Mark Peterson/Corbis; p. 47 © Underwood & Underwood; p. 51 © Peter Hvizdak/The Image Works; p. 54 © The Dispatch, Dan Videtich/AP/ Wide World Photos.

Designer: Evelyn Horovicz